FROM THE STREAM
TO THE OCEAN

FROM THE STREAM TO THE OCEAN

The enigmatic journey of Life

Parvati Variyar

PARTRIDGE

A Penguin Random House Company

To order additional copies of this book, contact
Partridge India
000 800 10062 62
orders.india@partridgepublishing.com

www.partridgepublishing.com/india

ACKNOWLEDGEMENT

My special thanks to my husband, Sethumadhavan, for being a pillar of support and for encouraging me to bring out my new collection of poems in print.

A warm thanks to my son, Anil, for being my sounding board.

To my sisters and brother and my husband's family who are always so generous to appreciate any step I take forward, no matter how small.

Finally, a heartfelt thanks to my loving parents who sacrificed much to ensure that I received a good education and the courage to think for myself.

FROM THE WRITER

Right from childhood I had a fascination for writing poems. Then, the subject matter was simple and uncomplicated like losing a tooth, beauty of a smile or the moon. Oh, blissful childhood!

Over the years as I became more aware of matters which touch human lives, my writing acquired a little more solemn hue. My interaction with students in school and college made me keenly interested in factors which influence their personality and attitude. The study of Economics drew my mind towards socio-economic issues. All this finds reflection in my poems.

I have classified my work under four sections in order to maintain continuity of thought.

The most significant segment of any country's population is the youth. The first section therefore deals with the hopes and aspirations of the youth, their goals and frustrations and the manner in which the general education system affects them.

To energize the youngsters, I believe, it is necessary to provide them a strong and stable emotional background. This is where the role of human relationships comes in. The second set of poems is thus about relationships which can be beautiful and magical in the best of times and rather painful and tricky when emotions turn sour. It is only when human bonds are nurtured that life takes a meaningful turn.

Life, to me, is an interesting and eventful journey. So, in the third section are poems which highlight the different facets of life including our thought process and attitude. I earnestly feel that if we are rational, tolerant, cooperative and considerate, we can jointly create a vibrant, beautiful world for ourselves and the future generations.

To really enjoy the roller-coaster ride, we need to value the society of which each one of us is an integral part. The concluding section, therefore, contains poems on individual and social behavior. The last poem 'The Joy Within' is particularly close to my heart as it is inspired by my loving and ever-generous mother.

Between the different sections I have inserted small poems related to Nature. I did so to emphasize that healthy, productive and prosperous human life is possible only if we are in tune with Nature.

Finally, a humble submission. If you find an extra pinch of suggestions or advice in the poetic content, my only line of defense is – once a teacher, always a teacher.

Contents

SECTION 1

Youth and Education

THE LEARNING PROCESS
(Is it possible to evaluate success in life?)

Teaching, the most basic of all professions
Mothers teach; fathers, siblings share their vision
Elders, neighbors shower advice, pitch in
Listening, learning, the young brain takes it all in.

Off to school one day, more teachers, more lessons
A new world opens up of reason and emotion
Varied subjects some difficult, some easy
Surpassing any computer the brain is busy.

Higher the education more intricate the study
To achieve specialization the mind is ready
Deeper and deeper the process of learning
Finally, is knowledge complete, the question burning.

On and on continues the frantic search
Some who aim higher step into research
To acquire intensive knowledge a great mission
Stretch the limits of knowledge to new horizon.

Tiring, challenging, this winding journey
The rewards for an aspirant often money
Opportunity, fame and status one of a kind
To quench the needs of body and mind.

Speeding to the top where is the time for thought?
How many assess what they added to their lot?
Caught in a whirlpool, emotional bonds swept away
Constraints and pressures take the breath away.

Education, job, salary, may fill the cart
But in the midst of plenty there is poverty in the heart
In a dense crowd lurks a fearsome loneliness
Evident sometimes, a clear deficit of life-worthiness.

When the race is over, who won is anybody's guess
Add up the cost, is there any true success?
Amidst the gloss and glitter and celebration
There is a long list of things that were never done.

☙ ☙ ☙

SET FOR TAKE-OFF

(The confidence of modern youth)

I am not a kid any longer
Childhood behind I am smarter and stronger
Confidently stepped into adulthood have I
With stars in eyes and head held high.

Capable am I to take decisions
The goals of life I can sketch with precision
With ability to see right from wrong
On my own steam I can gallop along.

Quite worldly wise I am sure I won't slip
Emboldened with knowledge at my fingertips
The technology-tool will my struggles lessen
Streamline my efforts and my life brighten.

Not much need for advice, out-dated it will be
To win the race new vision I foresee
The world has progressed but also shrunk so much
With anyone anytime I can be in touch.

What to make of my life I know best
For career options I need no test
Knowing my strengths and aptitude well
I can ensure my coffers swell.

ഌ ഌ ഌ

ACHIEVEMENTS

(Is there anything more to life than material success?)

I went to primary school and learnt the alphabets
Nursery rhymes I recited without a rest
To play with numbers I was taught
Reading, speaking, I felt I had learnt a lot.

Off to High School I skipped happily
Diverse subjects interested me greatly
Science and Humanities I read and grasped
Sports and music kept me enthralled.

Racing on to Senior Secondary
I put the first step towards my goal primary
A career in Medicine being my inclination
Devoured relevant subjects with concentration.

A special day indeed when I joined Medical School
With coat and stethoscope I felt so cool
After years of study and toil I graduated feeling proud
With my new status I stood out in a crowd.

More years of work rolled by unnoticed
In medical research notable breaks were accomplished
Treated hundreds of patients and earned goodwill
In my specialized field acquired fame for my skill.

Now in the twilight years of my existence
I wonder as I look through the life-lens
Education and career apart, what has been my gain
The real meaning of life have I ascertained?

Have I been a loving, caring child of my parents
To my children, understanding and tolerant
Towards family, society, country, have I done
Due justice to all my obligations?

Have I stood up for causes I believed in?
Have I been honest and true to the voice within?
Have I taken a stand at times of need?
Did I have the courage to match word with deed?

ര   ര   ര

TEST OF EDUCATION
*(Does the present day education system enable
the youth to handle real-life situations?)*

Many long years have flashed by
Since I stepped on the shore of my school
Reluctant kid to flamboyant youth
I have become dashing and cool.

Languages have I smartly mastered
Of society and law I have fair knowledge
Science and Mathematics are my forte
Varied my education, I acknowledge.

I stand now ready to boldly step
Into a new world challenging and wide
Interesting people, awesome experiences beckon
I need to take them all in my stride.

Will my education stand me in good stead
To handle life situations with balance and pride?
To know right from wrong and take a stand
To hold values upright and make truth my guide?

What use education if it only fills the purse
Adds to the ego and gives life some thrill
For the journey to be fruitful the heart must be touched
Only by sharing and serving can one race uphill.

～ ～ ～

ATTITUDE

(What matters ultimately is one's attitude to life)

Full of stress and strain is life
At every step problems at every juncture strife
From birth to death a journey challenging
Only right attitude can make it rewarding.

Studies are boring who doesn't feel
Most children will vouch it's a tough deal
But to get butter curd has to be churned
Without a little pain is anything worthwhile earned?

Some jobs are tough, time-consuming, some meaningless
Just for a salary they are tolerated many confess
A rat race, a pull and push to the top
But without competition whoever improved his lot?

Marriage is a gamble most people agree
Attraction may exist but of happiness no guarantee
Ego clashes and misunderstanding may occur often
But isn't success the result of risk well taken?

If life is cut short there are sobs and wails
Dreams remain unrealized and aspirations fail
But if long, fear of ill-health and loneliness terrible
Then, why measure life, just make it memorable.

ৎ৶   ৎ৶   ৎ৶

CALL OF THE HEART
(All that sparkles may not ring in happiness)

I longed to be strong, handsome and smashing
With a fine chiseled body like a Greek God dashing
Hours of effort, self-discipline and dedication
I attained my goal, earned great recognition

Looks of appreciation I received and also envy
Was showered with questions on my modus operandi
To keep up my striking physique I continued to slog
Afraid to fall from grace I never missed my jog.

I desired to increase my mental power
With the best brains in the world be at par
I read and analyzed whatever I could lay hands on
And topped exams as if to success born

Toast I was of the thinking community
Known far and wide as an awesome personality
Feted and honored for my enviable contribution
Every moment I strained to keep up my reputation.

I only wanted to know the true purpose of life
When peace is so blissful, why so rampant is strife
When life is transient, to accumulate why this craze
For wealth, power and fame, why are all in a daze?

I was hurt by the sufferings of people, the poverty
Shocked by the darkness in lives, the disparity
Wealth is only a means to help others I realized
Through kindness, love, my joy was maximized.

ᘓ ᘓ ᘓ

RESOLVE

*(If our inner strength is tapped, we
can attain the impossible)*

When memories hurt and the heart is scarred and heavy
and ingratitude stifles and worthless seems generosity
When the world seems callous and the people deceitful
and every good thought for others seems utterly wasteful
When insensitivity makes emotions a mockery
and decency is labeled inefficiency and foolery
When promises are loud and actions merely a shadow
and the world seems crazy and the future dark and fallow

JUST DROP

Drop the fears, the insults, the diffidence
    the taunts of the people that smart
Drop the uncertainty, the confusion, the reluctance
    which weakens the mind and heart
Drop the dependence, the weakness, the vulnerability
    which dampens the resolve, the goal

Drop the tears, the doubts, the frailty
    which strangle the music of the soul

AND GATHER

Gather the brightness of the sun
      which no cloud can darken
Gather the generosity of nature
      which no force can dampen
Gather the goodness of love
      which no hate can smother
Gather the strength of mountains
      which no tempest can shatter

Armed with mental and moral power, step forward boldly
If the resolve is true, you can touch the stars surely.

ౚ   ౚ   ౚ

NATURE IS BEAUTIFUL
Cherish It

A MORNING WALK

(A treat for the senses)

Early morning walk an impulsive decision
Turned out to be a treat, a vision
Meant to be just a healthy work-out
Filled the heart with joy without a doubt.

The wake- up call unique, a bird's song
Loud and clear it sang along
Up and down the musical scale
To herald the dawn in the sky so pale.

Eager to savor the experience new
On the soft ground soaked in dew
Briskly I stepped no time to laze
An awakening world my wish to embrace.

The air so cool and soothing to inhale
Fascinating to watch birds hop and sail
Flowers fresh on hedges and garden
Coconut palms swaying in gay abandon.

No honking of cars, no traffic jam
Pure and simple, everything peaceful and calm
Time stood still, miles moved on
If only such tranquility would linger on.

ॐ   ॐ   ॐ

SECTION 2

Relationships

A DEDICATION

(To parents)

The first recollection of an extended hand
To hold my little one and lead
When tears filled my eyes and was sad, morose
The warmth of a hug holding me close.

Growing up in the gentle embrace
Of parental love a great blessing
No matter what the pitfall the surety
That support and advice is a certainty.

The firm grasp of my father's hand
Symbolizing the rock-like support he stood for
The loving care and understanding of mother
Ever forgiving, ever ready to mould me further.

Parvati Variyar

Correcting my errors, instilling values
Teaching me lessons in fruitful living
Living models of hard work and integrity
Of courage and patience while facing adversity.

Lessons of living life as humans
With kindness and generosity, I learnt
Keeping materialism at arms- length, aside
To tread a balanced path I was advised.

Years have rolled by, life has changed
From body to spirit, life-cycle has revolved
Yet every moment their presence I enjoy
They live in my heart and confer infinite joy.

Whatever good I have imbibed in life
All derived from my parents dear
All achievements, talents, honor, feat
I offer with humility at their feet.

THE SPARK

(A thought for innocent children)

Innocent mischief, irresistible sweetness
Win all hearts with magical deftness
Giving to parents' life a new dimension
Effortlessly become the centre of attraction.

How wonderful if the fairy-tale continued
And the fruits of a happy union bloomed
Secure and loved in the warmth of the hearth
Children grew up to sanctify earth.

But when protectors turn predators
And love is shattered by hate
When quarrels, violence wreck a home-divine
The tender plant can only wilt and pine.

When insecurity and fear raise their heads
Confusion, frustration strengthen the dread
When the shield of family support wears thin
The ugly head of distortion rises within.

Helpless, unable to handle life's woes
At a loss, the troubled head bows
Friendless, isolated, distrustful and sad
Life's bow snaps in a moment bad.

Who is responsible for this tragedy?
Who could have changed the end for the good?
If concern was there for others' welfare
Would precious life be beyond repair?

◦◦ ◦◦ ◦◦

MY BEST BUDDY

Some relationships are unique

My first memory, a mini-sized creature
Two bright eyes his most notable feature
Tiny and helpless, with a piteous cry
Like a small cotton-ball with buttons for eye.

So soon its growth into a naughty little fellow
Here, there, everywhere, on my desk, under my pillow
My shoes, my books, my bag and my kites
All victims of its scratches and bites.

How I would rant when my plants were dug out
Angry and upset when all my rules he would flout
Then a glance at his remorseful face, my heart would melt
A great actor I knew, as at my feet he knelt.

Slowly, steadily, he has become my buddy
Anytime, every time, on my call he is ready
No meal is eaten without him by my side
No walk is complete without him running beside.

When off to school I go every morning
Woefully he sees me off at the railing
Later, one touch at the gate he knows I am back
So boisterous the welcome I often fall on my back.

Such a darling he is, so loyal, so much fun
Friend, protector, playmate all rolled into one
The terror of the neighborhood has such a gentle heart
My lovely labrador Tommy, from him I cannot part.

☙ ☙ ☙

ANCHOR

(In the name of friendship)

Cast in a special mould, a sincere well-wisher
Friend, a unique breed, life's best anchor
A shield to ward off life's blows and lows
A spark to brighten bleak days, disperse foes.

He is somebody who wins our appreciation
Understands our every mood, is an inspiration.
A patient listener when feelings spill over
Forthright, firm when mind changes color.

He talks sweet when the need is consolation
Acts tough when mood is procrastination
To further the cause, to ensure we awaken
No time constraints, all measures undertaken.

No matter what wealth a person may accumulate
Its value in the market will only fluctuate
A person who has friends is richer than any
Happier than the happiest, like a bee with honey.

A friend needs to be valued, he is priceless and rare
Friendship is a blessing, it must be nurtured with care
An emotional investment which safeguards our welfare
It is a treasure, so find time to catch up and share.

෨   ෨   ෨

MADE FOR EACH OTHER ?

(It is the essence that matters)

Of all the decisions the most vital
The choice of a life partner, a soul mate
To tread life's path as equals
The fusion of two distinct individuals.

Made in heaven or decided on earth
Marriage a vital turning point of life
For better or worse the story does unfold
In joy or frustration the future is rolled.

Lavish festivities, rapturous celebrations
Dashing looks, power, prestige or wealth
Cannot a successful relationship ensure
A harmonious blend is the real measure.

There is no gain without pain it is said
No achievement without real commitment
For a long journey of two minds to endure
Many adjustments have to be made to be sure.

Small arguments, disagreements add spice to life
Tears and smiles bring the drama alive
If one heart beats for the other when it matters most
The union is a blessing, worth cherishing utmost.

⌒ ⌒ ⌒

EASY SEPARATION

(Easy to break, tough to save)

Armed with degrees, confident, proud
Many seek jobs to stand out from the crowd
Interesting assignments and lucrative remuneration
Live life on their terms with satisfying elation.

Then comes marriage a fascinating union
Linked to another individual, a strange fusion
How will it shape life is often wondered
Will two paths meet to move ahead unhindered?

Personalities different and often equally strong
To understand each other and stride along
To handle the stress that comes their way
Patience and tolerance is needed day after day.

Parvati Variyar

Small fights and tears and debates rather long
Moments when everything seems to be wrong
But is any marriage perfect in this imperfect world
Isn't the experience of every couple sometimes blurred?

To sustain a relationship cherish it first
Come what may strive to keep up its worth
Through thick and thin, trust will grow
Adding strength to the relationship, love will glow.

 ∽ ∽ ∽

THE ILLUMINATOR

(A light to show the way)

At every critical juncture of life
Tensions arise due to uncertainty
What steps to be taken, what strategy used
So often the mind is utterly confused.

When at life's crossroads dire need is felt
To gain the support of a merciful mentor
Who with his knowledge and deep experience
Will guide and reveal life's essence.

Such a great teacher is verily God in human form
Endowed with spiritual power and Grace
Steeped in values, one who maintains equipoise
In the midst of problems one who can rejoice.

To find such a Guide is no easy task
He who gets such a preceptor is indeed blessed
Bowing to the teacher with utmost humility
Man can tide over all his ills with felicity.

In the material world he can retain balance
Resisting temptation he can lead a life secure
When the worldly obligations have been rightly fulfilled
To a higher plane he can rise anxiety stilled.

℘   ℘   ℘

NATURE SUPPORTS LIFE
Conserve It

CALL OF NATURE

(Pause and listen)

The weather was cool the breeze fragrant
The branches fresh and flowers vibrant
Every breath pure every step a pleasure
Made earth a bride, a veritable treasure.

Green fields lush, gently bowing fruit-laden trees
The fertile soil unpolluted, yielding generous bounties
Un-spoilt, untouched by greed of market and man
Blessed the nurturing hearts like only nature can.

When hands that tilled lost their grip, became lax
In the name of progress changed course, picked up the axe
The fields were filled and the forests cleared
The death knell of prosperity was surely heard.

In dry, concrete houses now people live and crowd
Dreams in their eyes, float around in a cloud
Reckless, without a thought for goals and deed
Unaware, the path of destruction cannot to success lead.

જ઼ જ઼ જ઼

SECTION 3

Life

THE LIFE CYCLE

(On and on it rolls)

The tiny fingers rolled into a fist
The cute mouth curved in a fascinating pout
The eyes closed tight in a sleep so restful
A sudden smile remembering the past blissful.

How memorable the moment when eyes first beheld
The little bundle of joy God's wondrous creation
So tender the feeling when arms held close the treasure
With the silent promise to love, nourish and nurture.

Don't all parents feel the same tug at their heart-strings
The same awesome sense of concern, responsibility
At a task tougher than any undertaken venture
For there is no criteria to measure success or failure.

Tough indeed life's unending minutes
Of their physical ailments and emotional woes
Of growing-up pangs and harsh world experiences
Toughest to see despair on their young faces.

Years race by over their milestones and challenges
Achievements to savor and shattered dreams to mourn
Education, employment, marriage and their off-springs
Events gallop by in a trice, winter to spring.

Soon, too soon, time takes its inevitable toll
Emotions still deep but the body does falter
Stumbling gait, bent back and memory rather fickle
Wrinkled hands extended to grasp ones more capable.

The supporter now a dependent, a reversal of roles
Eyes moist, vulnerable, less body more soul
The irrevocable journey chugs on and on
Towards the restful night does tread every morn.

 co co co

A GIFT TO CHERISH

(Life is short. Learn to value it)

A little flower, white and star-like
Dancing in the early morning light
Bright and radiant in bride-like joy
Catching my gaze it held me tight.

A little mud, some water and the generous Sun
Enough to make it bloom and sway
A little nurturing, a gentle touch of love
Its fragrance engulfed all in a spray.

But retaining its glowing youthful face
How long will it brighten hearts this way?
Soon, so soon, its charm will dull and fade
Wrinkled, weakened it will wither away.

Parvati Variyar

Short-lived indeed the gift of life
To scatter happiness and color far and wide
Before the clock ticks to an abrupt halt
Savour each moment, leave strife aside.

ဆ   ဆ   ဆ

A LOTTERY

(To accept- the situation or challenge?)

The great trials and tribulations finally over
Of confinement for long dreary months
Eventually released am I into a strange crazy world
Tottering on the rim of a nest, a little bird.

What fate awaits me I know not
In the mixture of fortunes, what will be my lot?
Some walk on thorns others on flowers
Who can say which carpet will be mine?

Will it be cuddles, love and caring smile
Sweet lullabies and joy to shorten each mile
With arms to support, hold me close
Shield from life's struggles and woes.

Or, will I be abandoned, shoved aside
To fend for myself, no one beside?
In a hostile world, cruel and cold
Isolated, unwanted, will I grow old?

No one to comfort me when I am down
Nobody to understand my tears, my frown
Watching the flashy world go by
Will I be sidelined, to heave and sigh?

No matter what, I will survive
Failures will strengthen me, not deprive
If luck passes me by, I'll toughen myself
In this jungle of mankind, I'll prove myself.

∽ ∽ ∽

TRANSIENCE

(A play of the pair of opposites)

Life- a beautiful, exotic bubble
Holding within flower and pebble
Lot of excitement and great happiness
A path of thorns and some dizziness.

Laughter and tears
Some blessings, some fears
Splash of color like dusk and dawn
Flash of hope when a day is born.

A unique play which contains all
To live it full, one must endure all
To value light, darkness must be borne
To enjoy success, failure the stepping stone.

ᥴᢥ ᥴᢥ ᥴᢥ

IMPACT

(Weigh the pros and cons)

Life is full of decision demanding situations
Big or small they are important occasions
Impact of some limited and temporary
Some others permanently etched in memory.

Where to study, what to study
Academic decisions are relatively easy
If error in judgement reversal is possible
With corrective action effects turn favourable.

To work or not to work and where
Important decisions, need thought and care
May boost up finances and independence
But increase mental stress, question life's essence.

Choice of marriage partner a very vital decision
Can create heaven on earth, a blessed union
Or in an existing stable happy environment
Can raise rough waves to everyone's detriment.

To start a family or not and when
Is a decision to be carefully taken
For if focus is on career and financial elevation
Years may flash by leaving life barren.

If blessed with children, life takes on a different hue
Sometimes a roller-coaster ride, sometimes a walk on dew
To coordinate family and career is an art intricate
Thoughtful decisions, timely moves, from stress extricate.

Retirement looms and old age beckons
How to hold on to the reins is the tricky question
If seeds have been sown right in the field of life
Peace and joy the harvest, without tears or strife.

ဆ ဆ ဆ

ROOM FOR LAUGHTER

(Notice the star in the blanket of darkness)

Most captivating, infectious, a peal of laughter
Full -throated, from the core the spontaneous splutter
Strengthens the heart, wipes away the lines
A smile the best way to overcome the whines.

Tough times may loom, there may be cause for tears
But in the saddest moment a smile can subdue fears
Don't roses bloom amidst thorns, in the dirt the lotus
Look, in this cruel world there is goodness around us.

When you see the hungry, notice the hands that feed
In the well of mindless violence, there are hearts that bleed
When values go for a toss and suffering fills the cup
When hope sinks rock bottom, know the next step is up.

At every juncture, corner - look for a reason to smile

In this fast-paced race of life – pause, relax for a while

There is nothing worth fighting for, nothing more precious
than life

When peace bestows greatest joy, why this need for strife?

ↄ   ↄ   ↄ

THE WRITER

(Scope for improvisation)

Who writes the chapters of our destiny
Traces the trails of life's journey
The background, the mental framework, the ability
Who paints in the colors of our personality?

Some born in fine houses wrapped in silk to the toes
Stepping stones of gems; uninterrupted money flows
Holidays and cruises, parties and passion
Every moment a reason for celebration.

Others work their way up in life with little song
Focused and ambitious, work hard and long
Targets and deadlines, no time to laze
No rest, no relaxation, so fast the pace.

Yet others just stagger around
Dead to emotions, in misery drowned
Hardship and darkness, so tough to cope
Stars and flowers not theirs to hope.

Is each role defined and un-changeable
Cut and dried, fixed and unalterable?
Then what worth the human creation
If the intellect is merely a decoration?

Immense is the power of the mind, let's know
To uplift and change the course of the flow
With balanced thought and honest evaluation
Fate can be modified through conscious action.

ɷ   ɷ   ɷ

THE REINS OF LIFE

(Shake off the fears)

From the forehead poured pure sweat
Hands clenched and unclenched, moist and wet
The heart beat was fast and disturbing
The throb in the head was hurting.

Life even when normal is stressful enough
When things go wrong it is frustrating and tough
Problems varied and complex attack like a virus
Finding solutions becomes a task tedious.

All say education will make life easy and secure
So I poured over books to make my path clear
Armed with degrees and certificates I was sure
Work and wealth would be round the corner.

Hope turned to despair as the wait did lengthen
All avenues explored but darkness didn't lighten
Sunday editions, websites, listed many vacancies
But for me, alas, there was no opportunity.

For some positions I was over qualified
For others had not the technical skills clarified
Some required more experience, documentation
Yet others offered inadequate remuneration.

Day in and day out I wracked my brains
To find for myself a suitable workplace with gain
While many around me seemed to pick jobs at will
For me there was no optimum place to fill.

Sad and depressed not knowing what to do
Slowly, unknowingly, into myself I withdrew
Closed in my room, glued to my laptop
I searched and browsed caught in a mind-trap.

Family was upset, observations flew
Criticism, blame, accusation- mostly untrue
He never took his studies seriously, some ranted
Sports and games are distractions, others commented

Job prospects must be considered before taking a course
Following 'life's dream' takes life off-course
A big gap there is between dream and reality
Head in the cloud can only bring misery.

Mother wrung her hands and quietly cried
He is such a good boy, his best he has tried
His time is unfavourable, luck not at his door
Or my dear son would be earning a crore

The astrologer has said the going will be tough
Problems and worries will make the years rough
Blessings of God by all means has to be sought
To overcome the obstacles and better his lot.

Suggestions and advice lashed like a storm
For days and months lectures were a norm
Afraid to face others, dreading pity and scorn
A recluse I became hiding from the dawn.

Then one day I decided enough was enough
I am not spineless to hide in a trough
My life is my own to mould and make
I will not allow it to disintegrate.

With newly found vigour and cool, positive mind
I scanned websites for work avenues of any kind
With patience and confidence I was sure
Within a week I would a job secure.

Three days gone I could call myself employed
Simple and ordinary but my joy was unalloyed
With sincerity and honesty I performed well
Giving the best of myself, my heart did swell.

A month later a raise was in store
Effort recognized, I was energized more
Knowing extra knowledge would better my prospects
Decided to gain expertise in relevant aspects.

Six months gone I had a new certificate to my name
Moved to greener pastures with better terms and fame
Assessed strengths and weaknesses through introspection
Shouldered responsibility to perform above expectation.

Five years later, highly qualified and skilled
A significant position in my field I filled
Enviable salary, status and all the works
A beautiful house, car and much higher perks.

Relatives and friends now valued me greatly
Came for advice, hung on each word fawningly
My worth soaring high in their impressionable eyes
Success made me a hero, a celebrity, in a trice

Amusing indeed the habit of people
To hail and laud when efforts are gainful
A twist of fate and laments grow
To weigh down a head which is already low.

Courage is needed to live life full
To move forward when situation is woeful
If mind is positive and effort concentrated
In the worst of times the heart is elated.

છ છ છ

WATER IS THE
NECTAR OF LIFE
Save It

OBLIGATION

(The future lies ahead)

The majestic ocean a sight to behold
Hides unfathomable treasures in its bosom cold
Miles and miles of water, awesome, boundless
Awakens a strange peace, a silence priceless.

Rivers flow on freely, merrily
Now fast, now slow, to join the ocean eventually
Bubbling along over mud, moss and stone
Grants happiness and joy to sorrow- prone.

Generous, selfless, the blessings of nature
Ready to meet the needs of all living creatures
Equal the right to enjoy its taste nectarine
Equal the duty to sustain without mine and thine.

For centuries it has nourished the plain and hill
Bestowed bounties on those who toil and till
Let us do our share to maintain its gracious flow
For ever and ever let its strength and purity glow.

இ இ இ

SECTION 4

Society

A HOUSE FOR SALE

(From a 'house' to a 'home')

When my house was constructed I never imagined
How maddening its future sale would be
The bungalow, my prized possession, my home
Such critical, scornful glances it would earn me.

Ignorantly confident its sale would be a sail
Happily I awaited a queue of buyers
Excited, enthusiastic, they would laud and hail
I thought they would come with cash in layers.

They came, inspected but their hearts were not conquered
Questions rained from all sides, sharp and hurtful
When, why, how - intricate details were required
Oh, for an elephantine memory, was my prayer pitiful.

Why the kitchen here, why the window there
Shouldn't there be more space to the East?
Why, oh, why the gate here and the door there
Verily, on a spray of ridicule I was forced to feast.

I staggered under the weight of queries
More questions than I had faced in my life ever
Morale in dirt, confused, drenched in worry
I thought my lovely house would be sold never.

I should have studied the whys and wherefores
Out-dated, irrelevant, worthless indeed my perception
In blissful ignorance I had lived on life's shores
Believing a home reflects the residents' vibration.

In this enlightened era of technology and education
The mind is still shrouded in superstition
Instead of applying rational thought to action
Matters are viewed with fear, farce and emotion.

Undue stress on glitter, pomp and show
The value of a house measured in tiles and flooring
Exotic paint, false ceiling and kitchen modular
Designer fixtures, expensive fittings and shiny railing.

Parking space for multi-cars a necessity
Decorative lights at every conceivable corner
ACs and geysers, inverters and solar panels
As added attraction, a fabulous home theatre.

In the midst of all this technicality and glitter
Is any place earmarked for human sentiments?
For fresh air, sunlight and cosy corners bright
Space for laughter and boisterous, happy events?

A house, grandiose or small, what does it matter?
Radiating the attitude and values of the family it enfolds
Simple, comfortable, it can still steal the thunder
And become a home of joy, more precious than gold.

ல ல ல

BUILDING OF CARDS

(Nature shows the way)

The little bird so happy and gay
To build its nest gathers twigs and hay
Industrious, focused, it toils along
Till its home is made, beautiful and strong.

The tiny ants pile mud on ground
Slowly, steadily, raise the mound
Months of effort produces an anthill
For them to burrow, rest at will.

The delicate seed unseen under the soil
Slowly emerges as a sapling royal
Years of growth the tree stands tall
Giving shade, flowers, fruits to all.

The bond of love so wonderful like spring
Between parents and children, friends and siblings
Years of trust, care and sacrifices galore
Relationships strengthen like heart-warming folklore.

Everything precious takes time to grow
The creative process is delicate all know
To nurture and maintain, patience is essential
Selfless effort and perseverance substantial.

Easy, so easy, to destroy and shatter
Home or trust, all that does matter
In one rash moment the card- castle tumbles
Years of fruitful action just vanish like bubbles.

Take care of thought, word and action
Knowingly, unknowingly, they can set off a reaction
Like fragile china handle with care
Be watchful lest there is little chance of repair.

∽ ∽ ∽

THE SUMMIT

(The view from the top)

Villages a rarity, new towns have emerged
The attractive simplicity in a fast world submerged
Cities are modern, dazzling and bright
Consumer is king and might is usually right.

Carts and bicycles have limited space
Exotic, sleek cars have taken their place
Flats and buildings have come up high nigh
A concrete jungle indeed, reaching out to the sky.

Education for money, status and fame
The teaching-learning process a materialistic game
Values, sentiment pay a heavy toll
To compete and win is the primary goal.

Relationship just a temporary alliance
On the buttered side is the safe reliance
He succeeds who is ambitious and clever
In an ever-changing world which bond is forever?

Personal life caught in a marsh
The journey to the top both lonely and harsh
At the time of exit, the final bow
What is gained, what is lost, who seeks to know?

ళ   ళ   ళ

PROGRESS ?
(The paradox)

What a weird world indeed we inhabit
Violence, hatred, distrust a habit
Struggle and suffering, a miserable life
Pain and death and increasing strife.

Technology touches heights yet millions starve
Medical research soars but does disease halve?
Towards Mars the gaze while earth is bled
Glaciers melt but waterless-life a dread.

Education on a high but ignorance grows
Millionaires turn billionaires, greater poverty woes
Speeches and lectures, a love for the talk
Sans love, sans trust, what's life's stock?

Towards more terrible wars why this march?
Between words and deeds why this mismatch?
Privacy lost, frauds galore, oh, what a mess
Dire need to curb the menace and re-assess.

Time to analyze, review abilities
Before condemning others, set right priorities
No strategy better than self-discipline
To pull out weeds, right effort the best medicine.

ༀ ༀ ༀ

THE RIGHT TO LIVE

(The bud will bloom)

Into the world I made my entrance
Hoping to fill my home with fragrance
Laughter, warmth and love will be my lot
A happy life I will lead I innocently thought.

Soon I realized I was not welcome
A girl does not a source of joy become
A burden, a nuisance, only to toil and please
In my own home no kind moment could I seize.

Why this difference, why this hate
Why do girls face such a miserable fate?
Aren't their thoughts and actions worthwhile
Don't they have even the right to smile?

I am intelligent, hardworking and gracious
Capable of shouldering responsibility, tenacious
Tolerance and patience I have in abundance
A happy woman is truly life's very essence.

As mother I love, as wife I care
As sister I pray for prosperity, welfare
With courage, originality, zest and zeal
I can scale great heights given fair deal.

Manage the home and serve my family
In the work place I can play my role calmly
The right to live my life I will not surrender
I'll prove to the world I am a leader.

℘   ℘   ℘

BEING HUMAN

(Show the way)

Doing my home-work one evening I saw
My mother feeding a little bird
It chirped and twittered and pecked away
The sight warmed my heart and made my day.

Returning from school, in the garden tank
I saw tiny ants struggling to stay alive
With a leaf and stick I scooped them out
Enjoyed bliss to see them up and about.

On the way home after shopping one evening
My son and I came across an old beggar woman
Weak and emaciated, her look was pitiful
My boy offered his chocolate, made my heart joyful.

Turning over the pages of the newspaper each day
My eyes flit over reports of killings and rape
Such cruelty, such mindless violence day after day
In the quest for frills has the heart lost its way?

Today out for my usual morning walk
Hoping to enjoy the cool fresh air
Rattled am I to see kids stoning a pup
Shocked to hear its piteous cry and whelp.

Before my stunned brain can react
Stop the cruelty, question their act
I see them stop and scamper away
For a strapping youth has stepped into the fray.

Moist my eyes as the pup moves safely away
Relieved that acts of kindness still endure
If elders and teachers the value of life instill
No hand will rise to maim and kill.

⌁   ⌁   ⌁

TAKE THE LEAD

(Five fingers make a hand)

Of one society, one country, we are members
Independent but inter-dependent for our needs
We need to work, cooperate and join together
In a necklace, like priceless, colourful beads.

No mission is impossible if we join forces
No problem that cannot be solved if minds meet
If we can crush the thorns and embrace the roses
United we can ensure success, achieve any feat.

What other countries can do, we can do better
A treasure-house of knowledge and talent we possess
Blessed with the foundation of a glorious heritage
We can chart an enviable path of progress.

Our youth are an asset, an indomitable power
With technology at their fingertips and values true
Vibrant and innovative, they can raise the bar
Propel our nation into an orbit new.

Let us practice tolerance and positivity in outlook
With love and tact weave joyfully our culture diverse
The same sanctified air of our motherland we breathe
With a unified effort let us lead the universe.

ॐ ॐ ॐ

THE JOY WITHIN

(The more you share, deeper the bliss)

It was a special decision I took that night
That set me on an interesting journey
To do as much good as I possibly could
To living beings, one or many.

Each morning I wake up with anticipation
To find recipients of my experiment bold
Sometimes, an old man looks dazed by traffic
Eagerly, I run up to help him cross the road.

My searching eyes locate an old woman
Weary and lined with a babe in arms
From my lunch- box I remove a sandwich
Happily drop it into her extended palms.

I give my old toys to children who have none
Clothes to those who need them more
Notebook and pencils, umbrella and bag
Some new, some not-so-new, but their spirits soar.

Each act makes my heart happier, lighter
When the great joy on their faces I see
Giving is any day better than receiving
The best lesson my Mom taught me.

As a kid I liked toys, bags and dresses
Waited impatiently for any special occasion
Birthdays, festivals, any other celebration
The gift I would receive, the only consideration.

Holding a beautiful bag one evening
Returning from shopping with my Mummy
Lurking behind a lamp-post I saw
A little girl gazing with envy at me.

No smile, she seemed peaked and hungry
Clothes were shoddy, her hair unkempt
The joy of my gift temporarily gone
Repulsed, I looked at her with contempt.

My Mom smiled and beckoned the dirty waif
Surprise and doubt the girl's eyes held
Gently Mom extended my favorite cookies
Stunned, thrilled, she came, grabbed it and fled.

Upset for giving away my cookies
I shook off Mom's hand and stamped ahead
Then, what made me turn back I do not know
To glare at Mom or at the pest she had fed.

Mom's face was calm, indifferent to my sulk
As my eyes swiftly swept the scene to locate my foe
There she was crouched under the old lamp-post
My favorite cookies spread on her lap and toe.

One by one, she popped them into her mouth
As if to fill the depths of hunger her need
Her eyes met mine as she munched and licked
For an instant a pause, then back to the feed.

A tug at my hand as Mom pulled me forward
But strangely locked was my eye to the scene
Surely, never had she tasted anything like this
Never had I such desperate fulfillment seen.

As I moved away one last time I turned
To see her pick up the crumbs scattered apart
Stuffing them into her mouth she looked at me
And gave a smile that is still etched in my heart.

So much joy the cookies could give I didn't know
I looked up to see my Mom watching me
Strangely happy that she had given my cookies to the girl
I grinned, hugged her warmly for educating me.

Years have flown and busy I still am
To do what I can for those less blessed
The most satisfying of all work I find
To bring a smile on a face woeful and stressed.

৲৹ ৲৹ ৲৹

ABOUT THE WRITER

Parvati Variyar is an Indian who has spent twenty-eight years in the teaching field. She has an M.Phil in Economics and has taught the subject in colleges in India. She studied English Literature while doing her Bachelor of Arts course and was happy when she got a chance to teach English to Secondary School students when she moved to Tanzania with her husband.

All along Parvati has enjoyed writing articles, poems and short plays and some of them have been published in local newspapers and magazines.

'From the Stream to the Ocean' is her first collection of poems to be brought out in book form.

She currently resides in India.

ↀ ↀ ↀ